BOB & AUDREY'S WAR

1st Edition

Published in 2021 by

Woodfield Publishing Ltd
West Sussex, England
www.woodfieldpublishing.co.uk

Cataloguing in Publication Data is available from the British Library

ISBN 978-1-84683-196

Printed and bound in England

Typesetting & page design: Nic Pastorius
Cover design: Klaus Schaffer

Source document:
Bob and Audrey's War - Ormrod (final).ppp

Bob & Audrey's War

THE EXTRAORDINARY EXPERIENCES OF A
YOUNG ENGLISH MARRIED COUPLE
DURING THE SECOND WORLD WAR

DAVID ORMROD

woodfieldpublishing.co.uk
Publishing Ltd
WOODFIELD
independent book publishers

Woodfield Publishing Ltd
West Sussex ~ England

For full details of all our published titles visit
www.woodfieldpublishing.co.uk

*This book is dedicated to
the memory of my parents,
Bob and Audrey Ormrod,
and to the members of the
French Resistance in Picardy
in the Second World War*

Bob and Audrey Ormrod, just married, May 1942.

This book records the remarkable experiences of my parents, who met and were married during World War Two.

My father, Bob Ormrod, joined the Army at the beginning of the War, but later switched to the RAF, trained as a pilot in North America, became a Halifax bomber pilot, was shot down over France on only his second Bomber Command mission, was sheltered by the French Resistance, captured and interrogated, endured four different prison camp regimes and survived a forced march, which culminated in a journey by cattle truck in the bitterly cold winter of 1945.

The wartime experiences of Audrey Partington began in August 1939, when she was head girl of Parliament Hill School in Camden, evacuated to St Albans in Hertfordshire, where she completed her final year of education in challenging conditions. She met her husband-to-be in 1941 and after a whirlwind romance they married in 1942. She went on to serve in the Auxiliary Territorial Service – ATS – gaining officer rank.

Though separated for much of the war, Bob and Audrey exchanged letters and their correspondence forms the basis for this book.

Bob &
Audrey's
War

Contents

Audrey in her ATS uniform.

Bob in his RAF uniform, proudly displaying his pilot's wings.

Acknowledgements

My first acknowledgement is to my parents themselves who inspired me to write this book and for all their lively letters, which were my main source. In 2015 I skimmed through the vast amount of papers left after my mother died and noted the bundles of war-time letters and other documents she and my father had preserved. I decided that this archive should be preserved and that I would write an account of Bob and Audrey's experiences for my children and future generations.

I appreciated that, understandably, there were few documents relating to the period that my father was sheltered by the French Resistance and set about finding out more. Through Suzanne Williams of our local twinning association, Pierre Mireaux was contacted and he in turn located Gerard Toron, who, as a child, had had to share his bedroom with my father in St Valery sur Somme in 1944. On our visit to Picardy in 2015, not only did Gerard take my wife Helen and me to his war-time home, but, among other events, he hosted a magnificent lunch for us with descendants of the local Resistance and next day a meeting with Cahon council. I am indebted to these named people and numerous other French men and women (some of whom are mentioned in my notes) for their interest and support. I was able to add what they told me to my diary account of a conversation with my father in 1989.

Over succeeding years I read through the hundreds of pages of my parents' letters and documents. I am grateful to my sister Kate, who sadly died in September 2020; she went through all the papers in her possession and found relevant ones to add. I then decided it would make my account a more interesting read if I selected just a few sentences from each of the letters, adding some extracts from non-fiction works to give a little historical context.

I want to express my gratitude to my family, especially my son James, and to the rest of the Ormrod clan for their help and support. Most importantly, I want to thank Helen for all her practical help with this book.

~ CHAPTER I ~

Bob Joins Up

Anyone seeing Bob and Audrey so content in their creative pursuits in the latter years of their lives, would have found it hard to believe what they had endured during the Second World War.

Bob was born in Kingston-upon-Thames on 25th September, 1917. He was named Harry Kenyon Ormrod, although in conversation he was always known as Bob. His father was Edward Harry Ormrod, who served in the Boer War and in the First World War, when he was a Sergeant Major Instructor in Musketry. His mother was Bertha Maude Nicholson, who had inherited a share in several properties in Oldham; she moved to the South of England and married Bob's father, whose family are understood to have also originated from Lancashire.

Bob had three older siblings: Elsie (known as Edwina) who became a nurse in the Second World War, Dorothy (known as Dods) who was a schoolteacher and Edward, known as Ted or Teddie in England, but known as Bill in New Zealand; he emigrated there in 1936, later becoming a surveyor and Provincial Grandmaster of the Freemasons.

Bob attended Tiffin School in Kingston. His school records show his conduct to have been "Good" (apart from one semester) and he passed his General School Certificate.

However, he left school at 16 and described having various jobs, one of which was attempting to sell vacuum cleaners. He later decided he should further his education and attended evening classes whilst working during the day.

In January 1939 Bob travelled to eastern Europe, where he supported himself teaching English, although sometimes his teaching was in exchange for German lessons. After a couple of months in Budapest, Bob moved on to Subotica in what is now Serbia, and in early July he moved on again to Romania. There he spent three weeks in Haţeg in Transylvania before crossing Romania to Constanţa, where he found a merchant ship from Liverpool. He worked part-time on board this boat, which was heading for England. Bob arrived home on 29th August, 1939, just five days before war was declared.

Within a few days Bob, together with Peter Waugh, his close friend from the athletics club Kingston Harriers, attempted to enlist in the Royal Air Force, but they were not accepted. Bob then volunteered to join the Army using the surname "Kenyon-Ormrod". Bob was the last person one could call snobbish, but it is believed he used this hyphenated surname in the hope it would enhance his chances of being accepted in the Royal Army Service Corps. Whether this had any bearing or not, Bob successfully enlisted for "the duration of the emergency" in the RASC at Acton on 15th September, 1939.[1]

Bob was issued with instructions in the event of a gas attack;[2] these included immediate action for "personal decontamination" which could be "done on the move": "Cotton waste – Remove free liquid on exposed skin. Ointment – Rub vigorously into exposed skin for at least ½ minute – using both hands."

Although not yet 22 when he enlisted, Bob recalled feeling out of place in his first dormitory with teenage volunteers.[3] He was briefly engaged as a physical training instructor, but was soon able to indulge his passion for cars and driving when he became an army driver. He had learnt to drive after leaving school before the introduction of driving tests.

Unfortunately, no records survive from Bob's time in the Army and, although he later showed himself to be a prolific letter writer, no letters have been found from this period. It is understood, however, that Bob was stationed in the Orkney Isles from the autumn of 1939 probably until early 1941. Bob wrote a poem describing service training there, which was later published in a local Orkney newspaper;[4] his handwritten note in the margin of a copy says it was "composed' in the car park in Stromness one sunny afternoon while waiting for a detail seated in a wee Austin". The poem describes a day at three hourly intervals, the 4th and last verses reading:

> Three o'clock. Out in the sun.
> Rifle drill. And the Lewis gun
> With its rat-tat-tat.
> Hot for this. But not all tripe.
> Although the order, "Slope pipe"
> Sounds a bit like it.
> Map reading next. Find a contour.

Mark the hill. What's it all for
Grumble the fellows.
Finding, marking. Asking, answering.
Six o'clock. Twelve hours past.
Free till morning. Now at last
Can rest and laze.
Cleaning boots. Polishing brass.
Off to the town. Might meet some Class
With sex-appeal Plus.
In the mess. With its N.A.A.F.I. beer.
Can sing some songs. Raise a cheer
For the leave to come.
Then back to bed. A quiet rag.
Last Woodbine. And bodies sag
Between the blankets.
Muttering. Puffing. Turning. Snoring.

Whilst serving on Orkney, Bob was very proud to have driven Winston Churchill, then First Lord of the Admiralty.

In October 1939, a German submarine had managed to enter Scapa Flow, where the British fleet was based, despite the belief that the entrance had been sufficiently blocked by sunken ships. The U-boat sank the battleship HMS *Royal Oak* and over 800 of the crew were killed.

Churchill travelled to Orkney to inspect the area of Scapa Flow. In order to block its eastern entrance, he ordered the construction of causeways between South Ronaldsay and smaller islands, and between them and the mainland of Orkney. These causeways became known as the Churchill Barriers.[5]

In 1941 Bob successfully applied to join the RAF; his number was 659144 and his earliest recorded daily rate of net pay was four shillings.[6]

On 27th October, 1941 Bob was ordered, after collecting "from the Cookhouse the unexpired portion of the day's rations," to report at the Air Crew Reception Centre at Lords Cricket Ground.[7]

Bob &
Audrey's
War

~ CHAPTER II ~
Love at First Sight

On 23rd December, 1941, by a remarkable coincidence, in a hotel bar in Brighton, Bob spotted across the room a couple, who ran a tobacconist's shop in Shepherds Bush, London, where he had been buying his pipe tobacco. They were Dorothy Herbst (formerly Partington) and her second husband, William Herbst. With them was Dorothy's daughter, Audrey Mary Partington. Bob hastened over to them and was introduced to Audrey. It was love at first sight and a whirlwind romance followed.

Audrey was born in Wembley on 7th September, 1921. Her mother was a senior nurse and her father, Wilfred Partington, was a writer and journalist. According to Wilfred's obituary in the *Times*, he was also 'engaged in secret Government work' in the 1930s. Audrey was an only child and the family, with their dog Mary, lived happily by the sea in Birchington, Kent. However, Audrey's parents' marriage was a tempestuous one and life became difficult for Audrey, especially after the family moved back to London when she was 10. Dorothy and Wilfred later divorced.

The Second World War began unusually for Audrey. In the summer of 1939, she was appointed Head Girl of Parliament Hill School in Camden, which she had attended since just before her 11th birthday. Audrey later[8] wrote that they were recalled to school at the end of August 1939; they enjoyed a heatwave in the extensive school grounds before the call for evacuation came. She described the day:

> "Excitement and anxiety were mingled as we marched out of the school gates and down the familiar road to Kentish Town. We each carried a small quantity of hand luggage and were securely labelled (a terrible indignity to the 17 and 18 year olds) and had in our care a great number of small brothers and sisters."

Unknown to the evacuees, they were originally destined for St. Albans, but the train ended its journey at London Colney, where:

> "...as it grew dark many of the school still stood lining the roads, as they had been for hours, while the staff frantically knocked up and down begging people to take us in. However, we did all eventually get a bed of some sort that night."

Audrey went on to describe how she and other seniors went on 3rd September, 1939 to the temporary headquarters of Miss Edmed, the school's headmistress. A member of staff was standing "in the doorway with a tea towel ... when Miss Edmed turned on the wireless for us to hear the statement of Mr. Chamberlain that we were at war – it was a solemn moment."

Audrey recounted how, when they moved to St. Albans,

> "Half-time schooling was organised with the grammar school. They used the building in the morning; it was ours

in the afternoon, and for the rest, lessons were held in huts, halls, pubs and fields – and we did a lot of walking."

By the summer of 1940 Audrey recalled "the whole evacuation scheme was collapsing around us. ... Parents longed for the younger ones to come home, billets were often only too anxious to be rid of us and the seniors began to feel that school was a restricting place when the country was at war. But Miss Edmed held us together by the sheer force of her personality; she labelled us 'The Old Contemptibles' and we each felt it was a debt of honour we owed to the school to stick it out in St. Albans," which Audrey did until the end of the school year.

After leaving school, Audrey went to secretarial college and then worked as an assistant to the renowned classicist and internationalist, Gilbert Murray, who had recently been President of the League of Nations Union.

In April, 1941 the War was dramatically brought home to Audrey's father. He sent Audrey a priority telegram, which read: "Phone me immediately Wimbledon 2495 German bomber down in garden".[9] Audrey went that day to see her father.

On 23rd January, 1942 – a month after she had first met Bob – Audrey enlisted in the Auxiliary Territorial Service [the women's section of the Army during the War] for the "duration of present emergency".[10] By 21st February, she was stationed at No.2 ATS Training Centre in York and issued with her uniform, "necessaries" and equipment, which included one steel helmet and helmet camouflage net.[11]

Audrey was deployed in several anti-aircraft units. She spoke of being stationed at Brighton and near Nettlebed in Oxfordshire, where she was in charge of an anti-aircraft battery. There were periods at Regimental Headquarters as a clerk on "general duties" and later in charge of records.[12]

It was not long after Audrey's first deployment that Bob proposed to her in a greetings telegram from Perth in Scotland:

> "Darling – feel like marrying cheesed off airman with dollar in bank – if yes, send ounce Murray's Mixture, if no, send sharp razor blade, trembling, Bob."

Audrey telegrammed back:

> "In lieu of ounce Murray's Mixture, Yours for ever and ever Audrey."[13]

On 14th May 1942, less than five months after they first met, Bob and Audrey were married at the Church of All Saints in the Parish of Hampstead. Audrey's father and Bob's sister Dods were the official witnesses.[14]

Bob and Audrey spent their brief honeymoon in Henley-on-Thames, not far from Nettlebed.

~ CHAPTER III ~
Pilot Training in North America

I n the first part of 1942 Bob had undergone initial flying training in Scotland – first at St Andrews and then at Perth – where he was second pilot on Gypsy Moth biplanes.[15] He completed his first solo flight in a Tiger Moth on 1st May 1942, less than a fortnight before his wedding.[16]

Just five days after the wedding Bob was sent to a Dispersal Centre in Manchester. He was among the last to be selected to train as a bomber pilot in North America under the Arnold Scheme[17] and was soon aboard a troopship bound for Canada. He wrote to his parents from "the Atlantic":[18]

> *You Pop, know what troopships are like, especially after nearly three years of war ... I long for a bed and a bath. I think I can safely say – without fear of dropping any bricks – that we are firstly staying in Canada a short while, then on to Georgia for the full course.*

Later in the letter, Bob wrote that the food was very good and that there have been "one or two lectures and very interesting too, being mostly talks by pilots off Ops." In a postscript he added: "Have a week's growth of 'fur' on my upper lip, so I think I'll cultivate it and call it a MOUSTACHE."

Bob sent a very long letter to Audrey full of reminisces[19] "written over a period of about a week" from "somewhere in the Atlantic – I hope!" He was relieved to have a mattress to sleep on rather than a hammock, as in rough weather he "fell asleep, immune to loud noises which [he] was told ... were chaps falling out of their hammocks." He also described wearing his cherished slippers "all day ...even on guard."

None of Audrey's letters to Bob has survived from his time in North America and only one letter from him to Audrey after he arrived there has survived. Bob wrote to her in an Airgraph (passed by the censor) from Moncton, New Brunswick[20], which he reached on 11th June 1942:

> "What a thrill it is to see lights in windows and along the streets after nearly three years of blackout; how marvellous not to have to queue, and even to stand in the street and just admire all the sweets, fruit and the full shop windows ... Only wish you were here too – you'd love it."

Bob wrote with similar enthusiasm to his parents about life in Monckton.[21] He described a common sight of "streamlined" cars "outside the camp waiting to take us out to view the sights or out to supper... Truly the people here are very friendly and hospitable, which after nearly nine months of RAF intakes, is a darn good show... Would I could have Audrey over here to enjoy it with me."

In his second letter to his parents[22] Bob mentions being impatient to resume his training, which was to be with the U. S. Army Air Corps in the Southern States of America. Meanwhile, he had enjoyed a "really wizard weekend by the sea, bathing and lazing around, just like the old days when the lads used to go down to the coast on the old bikes..."

In his next letter to his "folks"[23] Bob described a more disreputable occasion when he met three elderly female bootleggers in a dirty little cottage and haggled for a pint of rum, which tasted "like methylated spirits." He wrote later in the letter of seeing the American Clipper aeroplane: "Wow, what a kite to fly! I believe Churchill came over in it when he visited Roosevelt."

On 6th July Bob and his fellow trainees left Moncton by train for the United States. They arrived in Albany, Georgia on 9th July, 1942. Bob kept a printed menu[24] headed "Royal Air Force," which shows a hearty breakfast was enjoyed en route courtesy of the Louisville & Nashville R.R. Dining Car Service.

The trainees were stationed at Turner Field near Albany for a month, before they were moved on in turn to Southern Field, Americus, Georgia; Cochran Field, Macon, Georgia and Napier Field, Dothan, Alabama, spending approximately two months at each of these bases, as their training progressed.

The month's course at Turner Field included physical education, which left Bob in "almost agony to walk", but he was full of praise for the training. In a letter[25] to his parents he continued: "By the end of a month I am hoping to put on some weight in spite of the climate, as these Americans are very keen to get each cadet absolutely fit... They are even going to the trouble of dieting us specially."

Bob warned his parents that his letters would become less frequent, as he was on the course to achieve his "wings" which he had "wanted for years" and he had "no intention of failing." Nevertheless, as well as all his letters to Audrey and letters to his sisters, brother and friends, he wrote again to his parents under a fortnight later[26] expressing the hope "that there are not too many air raids over the home town" and enquiring how his father's bowling and billiards were going.

In his next letter[27] to his "folks" Bob described wanting to be alone on a Sunday and walking towards a town 23 miles away. His "first lift was given by three cheerful American soldiers in a ramshackle old two-seater ... a car not unlike my old Austin ..." His second lift was from an American Army Air Corps officer and his wife. They took him on "a most marvellous tour around Georgia" and into Alabama totalling 236 miles, returning him to camp at the end.

Bob went on to explain that that week they were "all moving to various flying schools, and there are concerts, parties and things in the camp as we are apparently the last class of UK cadets to be trained in the States." Meanwhile, he had "volunteered for a special class in calisthenics in order to try to gain some weight. In this climate! And after two weeks and a half I gained two pounds."

It was on 7th August, 1942 that Bob was assigned to Southern Field air base in Americus, Georgia. In a letter written a month later to his parents[28] he was ecstatic about having received eight letters and postcards the previous Saturday from Audrey, family and friends. "Mail and flying will always make me happy."

As to the latter, Bob said that he had "just come down from a two hours' trip alone – oh, dad, what a thrill to be up there all alone, with no one in front to criticize; and I'm sure I fly better solo, as I feel much more confident." Bob was flying a P.T. 17 trainer biplane with a 220 horsepower Continental engine.

Bob was in part responding to a couple of letters in which his father had said that Ted (Bob's brother) was believed to have been taken Prisoner of War in North Africa. Bob reminisced about times together before the War and "how we suddenly lost the elder brother complex; I long to be with him again." Bob's father had also told Bob that his mother was not well, to which Bob responded, "I pray that she is not too ill, and will soon be up and around, fussing in the kitchen."

Later in the same letter Bob wrote: "Oh, mother, I _am_ a lucky fellow having Audrey. Gee, I can't explain it but I have such a wonderful feeling within me, even though I am so far away, and long for her company. Her letters are absolutely wizard!"

Towards the end of this letter Bob said to his father, "...I can see you calmly walking about the house with no fuss whatsoever, 'doing' the blackouts ... giving mother medicine and so on. ... Assuredly the grandest father looking after the grandest mother, a fellow could pray for."

Although Bob was in North America for another six months, no other correspondence has survived from this period.

In late November Bob had a terrible shock – he received a letter informing him that his mother had died.[29] A letter written earlier, warning Bob that his mother was terminally ill, was not received until later. The death certificate of Bertha Maude Ormrod records that she died on 14th November, 1942 from malignant peritonitis and carcinoma of the cervix; she was 65 years of age.

There followed an incident of which Bob was deeply ashamed. After drinking heavily, he was with a group of fellow trainees when he set fire to an American flag. He was brought before a senior officer; it is understood that the latter knew of the sudden death of Bob's mother and this is the reason that Bob was let off with a reprimand.

Bob's behaviour on this occasion was more surprising in the light of the high esteem in which he held the American people; for example, he wrote of the American cadets and instructors, "I think they are grand fellows, so very frank and very humorous; and I like the business-like way in which they tackle every darned thing." [25]

In nearly every letter to his parents Bob also mentioned the tremendous hospitality of the local people. When stationed at Southern Field, Americus, Bob was particularly welcomed in the home of the Carswell family; when at Cochran Field, Macon, it was the Brooks family that took Bob under their wing and, when stationed at Napier Field, Dothan, it was the Harrison family.[30]

By Christmas 1942 Bob had progressed to an aeroplane with a 650 horsepower Pratt & Whitney engine; he was flying at night solo and in formation solo.[31] On 7th February, 1943

Bob performed combat aerobatics solo; these included loops, Immelmans[32] and barrel rolls.

On 16th February, 1943 Bob was awarded a certificate[33] that as an "embryo pilot" he had "satisfactorily completed a course of instrument flying ... without peeping." A week later Bob was presented with his Wings at a graduation ceremony and awarded a diploma[34] by the United States Army Air Forces confirming he had "satisfactorily completed the course of instruction prescribed for pilot training."

Bob sent a telegram[35] to Audrey in Marlow, Buckingham-shire:

> *"SPROUTED WINGS APPROXIMATELY 1000 HOURS 26TH BUT NO HALO EXCITEDLY THINE DARLING"*

A few days later Bob was back in Canada at Moncton before his voyage home to England.

Bob & Audrey's War

~ CHAPTER IV ~

Bomber Training for Bob & Officer Training for Audrey

Meanwhile in February 1943, Audrey was appointed a pay clerk "on ATS basic establishment of A coy 38 AA Bde (ATS) Group."[12] She was also made a Lance Corporal, but "unpaid at rank for 21 days".

On Bob's return from North America in March, Audrey and he were reunited after nine months apart. Both were granted leave and they stayed six nights at the Boston Hotel in Swan Road, Harrogate. Curiously, although they were married, the bill is itemized showing each of them separately; Bob is shown as paying 3d for a cup of tea, whilst Audrey paid an extra 6d for breakfast in bed on one occasion.[36]

Bob was first posted to the Personnel Reception Centre at Harrogate and then, in May 1943, transferred to the Advanced Flying Unit at Little Rissington, not far from Chipping Norton in Gloucestershire. As the War progressed, the station also stored aircraft received from the manufacturers prior to dispersal and had its own fighter force of Spitfires for their protection. (It was later to become the Red Arrows' home for a time).

At Little Rissington in June 1943, Bob, now a Sergeant, flew for the first time since February when he was in the

U.S.A. Initially, he was the second pilot (under instruction) of an Airspeed Oxford twin-engined trainer aeroplane; he made his first solo flight in the Oxford on 20th June. Whilst it is impossible to be certain, it seems likely that it was shortly before this solo flight that Bob was anxious and lacking in confidence until he received a "beautiful" and reassuring letter from Audrey. (Unfortunately, none of Audrey's letters from this period survive). In an undated letter[37] Bob replied to his "wizard woman":

> "And to feel you right beside me is a comfort I did not fully appreciate until I needed you. I _know_ that this week will turn out all right, but I also know that, were it not for you dear, it doubtless wouldn't have done. ... Darling, don't worry, I'm not going to do anything foolhardy, and I promise you I shall not go up unless I feel safe."

In the same letter Bob wrote that that morning he took three exams and later was sitting puffing at his pipe reading "Smoke Rings and Roundelays," a eulogy on smoking (subtitled "Blendings from Prose and Verse since Raleigh's Time") selected and annotated by Audrey's father, Wilfred Partington.[38]

In the second part of this letter written at 7.30 pm, Bob described the Sergeants' Mess being "mucked around" for a dance that night. The usually sociable Harry Kenyon-Ormrod decided against " inviting some poor unsuspecting WAAF to flit around" with him; at Little Rissington he said he preferred to go out alone, rather than with his fellow airmen and that night contemplated going out for a drink "tout seul" after supper, to the nearby village of Chadlington.

It was also about this time that Bob sent Audrey a telegram congratulating her on being promoted to Corporal[39] and thanking her for "one year of Heaven."

In August, 1943, Bob was posted to No.19 O.T.U. at Kinloss[40] on the Moray Firth[41]. Here pilots and crews of bombers were trained for operations. There were numerous fatal accidents during training, which have been attributed to worn-out aircraft and "the youthful inexperience of their crews ... some classes lost as many as 25% of their strength in three or four months."[42]

At Kinloss Bob made his first flight as first pilot in the twin-engined Whitley V. By 23rd September, he had completed 12 drills abandoning Whitley aircraft by dinghy and 12 drills by parachute[43] and was soon practising simulation bombing with his crew. At the end of his time at Kinloss Bob's ability as a pilot was assessed as "average". It is not known how his fellow trainees scored!

In December, 1943 Bob was stationed at RAF Riccall, three miles from Selby in Yorkshire. This was a "conversion unit" where crews who had trained on medium bombers learnt to operate heavy bombers. Bob transferred from the twin-engined Whitley to the four-engined Halifax.

The Handley Page Halifax was a very large aeroplane with a wingspan of over 100 feet (over 30 meters) – wider than a Boeing 737 in its earlier versions. Despite its overall size, conditions were cramped for the crew; for example, the wireless operator was seated under the pilot and had to be seated first. The Halifax had a crew of seven comprising the pilot, navigator, the bomber, the flight engineer, wireless operator and two machine-gunners equipped with Browning machine-guns. Sometimes there was also a pigeon on board to take a message back to England in the event of a crash.[44]

The Halifax was built in sections, which made it suitable for production in small factories – 41 at the peak of production. A staggering 6,177 were produced in all between 1938 and 1946.[45]

In his next extant letter dated 23rd December, 1943[46] Bob wrote to Audrey that he was about to go to night vision practice: "Good fun, playing table tennis, netball etc with dark goggles on – and also doing tests." Bob lamented that they would be apart for Christmas again and talked about "pinching a kite" and flying down to the aerodrome near Seaford in Sussex – Audrey was in Brighton at this time.[47] Any meeting at Christmas must have remained a fantasy, as the menu[48] for the five course Christmas Dinner in the Sergeants' Mess at RAF Riccall has survived.

On 25th February, 1944 Audrey attended interviews, including one with a psychiatrist, to determine whether she was suitable for officer training. Bob wrote:[49] "it's grand to know you'll feel treated fairly whether you pass or not." Later in the same letter he mentioned he had some oranges for her.

In the next letter that has survived[50] Bob wrote congratulating her on being successful. Bob went on to explain the difficulty in arranging leave together. If the weather was not too bad, he would be assigned to a squadron for operations. If the weather deteriorated, he would remain at RAF Riccall. However, Audrey and Bob were granted contemporaneous leave and met in Yorkshire for 24 hours. Bob wrote:[51] "Darling, you've no idea how happy I am being married to you. I feel so contented after that beautiful 24 [hours' leave] and long for the next." Bob's crew navigator, Les Lambourn, was disappointed to have missed meeting Audrey at the end of this leave, but "anyway I met him at York and we travelled back to Selby together, and he took me on his crossbar back to camp..."

By a happy coincidence, Audrey was posted to Pontefract, Yorkshire for a pre-OCTU (Officer Cadets Training Unit) course, which began on 11th February, 1944. Just a few days later Bob learnt that he had been assigned to 578 Squadron, a recently formed squadron, which had become fully operational at Burn less than a fortnight earlier. RAF Burn was even closer to Pontefract than Riccall. After a 'phone call from Audrey, Bob wrote[52]: "When we get to Burn darling, and I have a bike (as I understand we are issued with them) I'm hoping I shall be able to nip over to see you most evenings..." He explained that he expected to be a while at Burn adapting to the new type of Halifax aircraft; this was a switch from the 1150 horsepower version with a Merlin engine to the Mark III Halifax with a 1615 horsepower Hercules engine.[16] It transpired, however, that Bob had very little time to adjust to the Mark III.

From Audrey's phone call Bob gauged that the first few days of her course had been tough and he wrote encouraging her. (Audrey said one of their tasks was cleaning several lavatories to eliminate from the course any cadet who thought this was beneath her dignity.)

He expanded on his own encouraging news:

> "All of us got pretty good [reports] but Les's was really super. He is surely a gen[ius] navigator and will be the greatest asset to us. As I remarked, I was recommended for a commission but of course that does not mean I've got it..."

The 578 Squadron crest.

~ CHAPTER V ~

Operations

O n a couple of occasions after his transfer to RAF Burn, Bob said it had been "super to be able to nip over to the flix with you and I've adored the last two evenings. ... Even last night I was as happy as a sand-boy, doing a spot of walking, singing to the whole wide world. We <u>are</u> lucky, angel, being so near ..."[53] Bob wrote the time "7pm" at the beginning of this letter and explained that he was on stand-by, although expecting a "scrub." He was sorry Audrey had waited in vain.

Ironically, Bob did fly that night – as second pilot on his very first op. with Pilot Officer Horsey as first pilot, on a bombing raid to Leipzig.

> *"On 19/20 February a force of 823 bombers, 255 of them Halifaxes, were sent to Leipzig. It was an ill-fated operation from the outset with only a part of the German night-fighter force being drawn off by a diversionary raid on Kiel Bay ... Harassed all the way to the target by night-fighters, the bombing force arrived early due to incorrect wind forecasts ... In all, 34 Halifaxes and 44 Lancasters failed to return, a staggering 9.5% loss rate."[54]*

Bob would not have been permitted to write to Audrey about the Leipzig mission, but in a letter to her on 22nd February, 1944[55] he looked to the future and the return of his navigator, Les, so that they "could get this wretched cross-country [flying] finished."

Later in this letter Bob wrote of his "most urgent piece of news: ... Tonight I sat in an armchair and sewed on my stripe more securely (I hope) also a button." At the end of this letter, he sought to encourage Audrey: "Keep up the old hard work – and don't let 'em get you down. Take care of your chilblains and chapped legs angel, won't you."

Two days later Audrey and Bob planned to go to the cinema together, but it was not to be.

Allied commanders were agreed that the invasion of mainland Europe would not succeed without first achieving superiority over the German Luftwaffe in the air. The Americans took the view that the best strategy was first to destroy as many as possible of the factories making aircraft and their equipment. Air Marshal Arthur Harris, Commander-in-Chief of Bomber Command (known as "Bomber Harris"), however, did not consider his force could effectively hit small urban targets in Germany and it required "a special directive"[56] before Bomber Command took their part in the huge Anglo-American offensive, which later became known as "the Big Week."

On 24th /25th February, 1944, Bomber Command's targets were the factories of Schweinfurt, a small city in northern Bavaria. Schweinfurt was then the leading place in the whole of Germany for the manufacture of ball-bearings, which were required in the production of aircraft, tanks and other equipment and thus crucial to the Nazi war machine.

Pilots generally only commanded aircraft on bombing raids after at least three operations in which they had flown in crews as second pilot. The Americans, however, were keen that the raids on Schweinfurt and elsewhere were massive. Hence Bob came to be the pilot of his Halifax in the raid on Schweinfurt that began on 24th February, after flying in only one operation previously.

Bob's crew comprised Pilot Officer Les Lambourn, the navigator (referred to by Bob in letters) from Tresco in the Isles of Scilly, Sgt. Tommy McCall, flight engineer from Dumfriesshire, Sgt. Stewart, lower machine-gunner and another Scot (from Wick), Sgt. Wilby, radio operator from London, Sgt. McCord, higher machine-gunner also from London and Sgt. P B McLaughlin, bombardier.

On 24th February Bob would have attended a preliminary briefing at 2.30 pm, which was followed by a meal and a later main briefing[57] before he and his crew got dressed in their bulky flying gear. Although the ground crew would have thoroughly prepared the Halifax, the flight crew carried out their own checks, which, for the pilot, included checks on a vast array of instruments and gauges.

The aircraft from RAF Burn flew south to assemble over Southern England in a cohort of 554 Lancasters, 169 Halifaxes and 11 Mosquitos.

"The whole combat force typically extended for 20 miles, was six miles wide and flew in staggered formation, the highest aircraft some 4,000 feet above the lowest. Crews had

to fly low over England, then climb to 14,000-15,000 feet, then increase speed and fly at 18,000 - 20,000 feet for bombing..." [58]

Crews also had to contend with intense cold – minus 35 degrees centigrade that night at 6,000 feet.

On the Schweinfurt operation Bomber Command "introduced a new tactic with the 734-strong force split into two waves with the first wave of 392 aircraft followed two hours later by the remaining 342."[59]

The first wave flew on southwards, crossing the French coast in Picardy. Shortly after turning eastwards towards the German border, disaster struck. Bob's Halifax was hit by fighter or, more probably, anti-aircraft fire. The aeroplane was lurching and losing height. Bob gave the order to his crew to bale out. He then managed to gain some measure of control of the aircraft, but his crew had already jumped from the Halifax. However, it was impossible for one person alone to land a Halifax, owing to the poor visibility for the pilot. Bob was left with no alternative but also to bale out – and pull the ripcord on his parachute.

Irwin Caterpillar Club pin, awarded to aviators saved by an Irwin parachute.

~ CHAPTER VI ~
Sheltered by the Resistance

B ob's parachute landed him in a field. He suffered a bruised ankle, but nothing worse. It was bitterly cold. He folded up his parachute, but the frozen ground was too hard to bury it, so he hid it in some bushes. He made his way to a nearby cottage on a smallholding, and risked the consequences on both sides by knocking on the door; it was opened by Monsieur Degeurville, who wore a traditional nightcap on his head. The kind Frenchman bathed Bob's ankle and directed him to a bed to sleep, next to a very frightened young boy!

Bob's Halifax crashed in marshy ground at Gouy by the village of Cahon, which is about 7 km west of the centre of the cathedral town of Abbeville. The exact spot was identified by the people of Cahon.[60]

It is believed that M. Degeurville's smallholding, which Bob left next day, was also near Cahon. Local tradition has it that Bob walked along the nearby railway line. At some stage on his trek he encountered some German soldiers. He described resisting the temptation to run for it, said "Guten tag" and walked on – presumably by this time Bob was already wearing the clothes of a Frenchman!

It is not known how or when Bob first met up with the Resistance, or the order and length of stay at the next couple of places. It seems likely that he was next sheltered for a few days by Monsieur Alexandre Mangeot at his farm at La Molliere, about 3km north-east on the road from Cayeux-sur-Mer. What is known about M. Mangeot is that he was illiterate and notable for his family of ten children.[61]

Bob was moved on to the home of Monsieur Julien Toron, Resistance chief for the canton of St Valery-sur-Somme. He and his wife, Thérèse, lived in the Rue du Chantier in this historic town.[62] Bob shared a bedroom with their two children, Michel aged 13 and Gérard aged 7.[63] Michel remembers their father using a knife to cut a spyhole from their bedroom to the ground floor, so that he, Gérard and Bob could look down and see who entered the house. Gérard, in particular, enjoyed conversations with Bob, who was relatively fluent in French.

Whilst in St-Valery-sur-Somme, Bob was also helped by Monsieur Louis Ricard, who owned the cheese dairy in Rue de la Ferté.[64] Gérard Toron was told that M. Ricard drove Bob in his van to Albert, a town about 85 km east of St. Valery and a Resistance rallying point. Bob was dressed as M. Ricard's assistant. There Bob was reportedly overjoyed to meet all but one of his crew members and, after an affectionate meeting, was driven back to St Valery.

The missing member of Bob's crew was Sgt. Tommy McCall, the flight engineer. In a heart-breaking letter to Audrey in December, 1944[65] his mother wrote that she had just received a letter from the Air Ministry that they "propose to presume that Thomas is killed for official purposes... Do you know if

Thomas was able to bale out with rest of the crew? If he did there is always the hope of him being in hiding somewhere."

Meanwhile, Tommy's body had been found in a meadow near Cahon. It is not known why, but his parachute had not opened. Sgt. Thomas McCall is buried in the Commonwealth War Graves section of Abbeville Cemetery; on his gravestone are written the words: *"Until the day breaks and the shadows flee away."* Tommy was just 20 years of age.

The surviving five of Bob's crew became Prisoners of War. Brian Mclaughlin and Ben Stewart were both in Stalag 357 near Thorn, which is now in Poland; earlier in the War it had been a prison camp for captured Army personnel. A.C. Wilby and A.J. McCord were both in Stalag Luft III near Sagan; this was the celebrated "Great Escape" camp.

By the end of February, 1944 Bob was in his next hiding-place in Gamaches, a village on the River Bresle, 6 km south-east of Eu. Bob was taken to the home of Monsieur Jacques and Madame Arlette Baillet in Rue d'Abbeville and was shocked to be told:

> *"I am very sorry I cannot offer you the best bedroom, Monsieur, but the Boche has it. I can make you comfortable in Gran'pere's room downstairs; he is a little strange at times, but he was tortured by the Germans." (Bob's translation[66])*

Bob recalled asking nervously: "Do you mean that a German is actually living here?" Bob's translation of the reply read:

> *"Ah, do not worry, Monsieur ... As long as you are quiet when he is in, he will never guess. ...Jacques has made a hole*

in the wall at the end of the garden and he will tell you how
to disappear if it should be necessary."[67]

When Bob was introduced to Jacques' and Arlette's baby daughter, Jacqueline, gurgling in her cot, he was told: "Ah, Monsieur, she likes you already; she cries when the Boche tries to be friendly."[66]

Bob continued his account:

> *There followed ten days of homely French life; eating eggs*
> *supplied by the German; listening to the BBC; the traditional*
> *hot brick from the oven in my bed; and evenings out, when*
> *Madame took me to visit other airmen hiding in the village,*
> *holding my arm and chatting gaily as we passed German*
> *sentries. Ten days of slipping behind doors or crouching under*
> *my sheets when the unwelcome lodger polished his boots on*
> *my window-sill; rigid behind a newspaper if he unexpectedly*
> *entered the room.*

Bob commented:

> *"When I expressed concern for their safety, the reply was*
> *a laugh, and yet their punishment would have been death;*
> *mine only a prison camp. But they did not hesitate."*

Among photographs posted to Bob by Arlette Baillet after the Liberation are a couple showing a group, which included Bob posed with an axe about to chop wood. The photographs are dated by Arlette on the reverse 12th March, 1944[68]. Arlette wrote to Bob after the Liberation[69] and Audrey replied on Bob's behalf, which led to an exchange of correspondence[70].

On 13th March, 1944, Bob and two Canadian servicemen were taken south by the Resistance and they headed for the

Spanish border. Their vehicle was stopped by German soldiers and Bob was interrogated. He maintained he was a Frenchman for three hours, but then made a silly mistake saying in French that he had done his National Service at the age of 10!

Unfortunately, Bob was carrying on him a photograph of the Baillet family, but he refused to divulge their names and whereabouts. That same day – 13th March, 1944 – he was taken to Lille and first imprisoned there.

On 15th March 1944, in St-Valery-sur-Somme, Gestapo agents came looking for Julien Toron. He later wrote he had been betrayed by "mauvais Francais".[71] Two Resistance fighters shot at the Gestapo officers, who took flight. Thérèse Toron telephoned to warn Julien, who was working on the railway at Noyelles station. Julien fled immediately and went underground with the Maquis. Meanwhile, his sons, Michel and Gérard, fled their home through their bedroom window[72] and over the garden wall.

The boys were taken to live with their uncle and his wife, and six cousins, on their farm in the Aube department. The boys were not treated particularly kindly by their aunt; they had to work hard – Michel looked after the cattle and Gérard cut wood – but they were kept safe. Their father Julien was in hiding nearby and able to see them fairly often, but the boys had to pretend that their father was a stranger, which they found tough when they were so unhappy.

In St-Valery-sur-Somme, the Gestapo agents returned and arrested Thérèse Toron following the attempted murder of their officers. She was taken, with three other women, and deported to Bergen-Belsen concentration camp, where they were incarcerated for 14 months until the camp was liberated by the British on 15th April 1945. She was found in an appalling state, living among the dead, having lost 20 kilograms in weight.[71] Remarkably, not only did she survive, but so also did the other three local women, inspired by the older Thérèse who, for example, made them eat raw turnips to stay alive.[72] The youngest, who was just 18, said that Thérèse was her "second mother."

Julien returned to St. Valery as soon as the town was liberated on 16th September, 1944 to find that his home was empty; all the furniture, linen and crockery had been looted by the Nazis. Julien had to wait another eight months before he learnt that his wife was alive. The family was then finally reunited; "What joy we had finding ourselves all together again as a family, safe and sound after a cruel separation".[71]

~ CHAPTER VII ~

Prisoner in Brussels

After five days in solitary confinement in prison in Lille, Bob was sent to the notorious St. Gilles prison in Brussels. This is the prison where Nurse Edith Cavell was imprisoned and later shot by firing squad in the First World War. In the Second, many of the prisoners were connected with the Resistance and Bob faced further interrogation by German officers, who were looking for him to divulge information about the people who had sheltered him. Bob held out, giving only the basic name, rank and number in accordance with the Geneva Convention.

Bob wrote in a letter to Audrey that he was "eating a lot of sprouts" in the hope that this clue to his whereabouts would get past the censor, but the letter never reached Audrey.

A note written by Bob[73] dated from 18th March to 11th May, 1944, simply reads "3 RAF". It is not known whether Bob was in a cell with three other RAF prisoners. Bob recorded in the same note that on 11th May he was placed in solitary confinement; he attempted to describe in verse[74], among other things, his routine:

And how do I pass each weary day?
Well, there aren't many things to do.
With my home-made cards I often play,
Although the games for one are few.

And in verses 6 to 8:

> *There's PT in the morning*
> *That's before my coffee and bread;*
> *Tho' I usually leave it yawning,*
> *'Cos I much prefer my bed.*
>
> *I'm pacing up and down a lot*
> *And sometimes walk outside.*
> *Though the yard is small, it matters not,*
> *For the birds and wind are my guide.*
>
> *Air raid alarms, an odd cigarette,*
> *Weekly shave, fortnightly shower,*
> *And all the food I can get,*
> *All help to pass each tedious hour.*

Bob's same note[73] says: "29.5.44 – 17.6.44 'CACHOT'" literally meaning "dungeon".

The exact sequence is not clear, but it is understood that Bob's note: "24.6.44 – 11.7.44 3 Belgians" referred to the period when Bob was in adjoining cells with Belgian prisoners. Bob communicated with them by tapping in Morse code in French on the pipes running through the cells. The prison guards discovered what was happening and suspected Bob was trying to escape. As punishment, on 11th July, 1944 Bob was again put in solitary confinement and was left in his cell without light for several days. He was, however, never tortured or beaten and was struck on only one occasion – for failing to salute a German officer.

Audrey with O.C.T.U. training colleagues.

Audrey with her "Q" staff

Bob and some of "C" flight at Cochran Field, Georgia, 15th Dec 1942.

Bob's certificate from the U.S. Army Air Forces for flying blind.

Blind Flight

SOUTHEAST AIR CORPS TRAINING CENTER
NAPIER FIELD, ALABAMA

This is to Certify that embryo Pilot Harry Kenyon-Ormrod has satisfactorily completed a course of Instrument flying, on this 26th Day of February 1943, in "The Jeep" without Peeping.

Capt. S. D. McDardale, Jr.
INSTRUMENT OFFICER

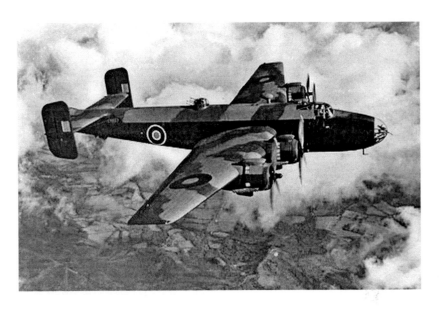

A Handley Page Halifax Mk III B four-engine bomber, the type piloted by Bob.

YEAR 1944		AIRCRAFT		PILOT, OR 1st PILOT	2nd PILOT, PUPIL OR PASSENGER	DUTY (INCLUDING RESULTS AND REMARKS)
		Type	No.			
						TOTALS BROUGHT FORWARD
FEB	31	HALIFAX B		P/O MOUNT	SELF & CREW	CONVERSION
FEB	19	HALIFAX B		AC INSTR?	SELF	LEIPZIG N.
FEB	22	HALIFAX B		SELF	CREW ...	CONVERSION
FEB	23	HALIFAX B		SELF	CREW	CROSS-COUNTRY
FEB	24/25	HALIFAX B	W	SELF	CREW	SCHWEINFURT op
						shot down over France on
						way out. 3 killed. P/L
						killed.
						(autograph)

The last page of Bob's **Pilot's Flying Log Book**.

Bob chopping firewood with the Baillet family, 12ᵗʰ April 1944.

Bob holding a very young Jacqueline Baillet.

CHRISTMAS 1944

Menu

ROOM 12
BLOCK 49
STALAG L.7

BOB

BREAKFAST

Orange Juice
Porridge
Egg on Toast
Prunes & Cream
Coffee

MID-MORNING

Corned Beef Sandwiches — Cocoa

LUNCH

Mixed Grill
Potatoes
Prize Bread

Raisin Cake — Tea

MID-AFTERNOON

Spam & Cheese Sandwiches
Wafers & Jam — Coffee

DINNER

Soup
Venison
Baked Potatoes — Mashed Potatoes
Carrots
Christmas Pudding & Cream
Tea

SUPPER

Cheese Bread & Butter
Jam Tarts — Cocoa

Bob's menu for Christmas 1944 at Stalag Luft 7.

Bob's 1947 painting of the Forced March.

~ CHAPTER VIII ~

A Widow's Pension

The day after the night Bob's 'plane was shot down Audrey received a telegram[75] at the ATS Training Centre at Pontefract;

> "*DEEPLY REGRET TO INFORM YOU THAT YOUR HUSBAND ... FAILED TO RETURN FROM AN OPERA-TIONAL FLIGHT THIS MORNING LETTER FOLLOWS PENDING WRITTEN NOTIFICATION FROM THE AIR MINISTRY NO INFORMATION SHOULD BE GIVEN TO THE PRESS*".

In a brief note[76] written later Audrey mentioned that she and Bob "were finally getting to the pictures" the night she received the telegram, but "There was me desolate in a Barrack room in Pontefract & Bob having parachuted into France was thinking about home & trying to hide and escape capture!"

It was over a week later that Audrey was sent the promised letter[77] from the Air Ministry, which said that Bob was "missing as a result of air operations on the night of 24th/25th February, 1944, when a Halifax aircraft of which he was captain set out to bomb Schweinfurt and was not heard from again. This does not necessarily mean that he is killed or wounded, and if he is a prisoner of war he should be able to communicate with you in due course. Meanwhile enquiries are being made through the International Red Cross Committee..."

A notice[78] received by Audrey included the warning to relatives that:

> "Any premature reference in the Press to those reported missing may jeopardise their chances of evading capture, if they have survived without falling into enemy hands."

Another notice[79] assured relatives that reliable news would be passed on at once and continued:

> It would be cruel to raise false hopes, such as may well be raised if you listen to one other possible channel of news, namely, the enemy's broadcasts. These are listened to by official listeners, working continuously day and night. The few names of prisoners given by enemy announcers are carefully checked. ... The only advantage of listening to these broadcasts is an advantage to the enemy.

On 6th March, 1944, the Group Captain commanding RAF Burn wrote a letter[80] of sympathy to Audrey and explained that "an Officer was specially detailed to collect [Bob's] property from his quarters early on the morning following his failure to return" and a search had been made of the Sergeants' Mess and locker room. Bob's personal property was to be sent to the RAF Central Depository in Buckinghamshire.

Audrey appears to have replied to this letter, sending her good wishes for the Squadron and asking for the names of the next-of-kin of the other members of Bob's crew. The

Wing Commander commanding No. 578 Squadron replied[81] with the names and addresses, offering any further assistance and expressing his sorrow "that there is as yet no news of your husband, but I am sure you are, like us, still hoping."

The cumulative effect of these communications, on top of the initial shock, can only be imagined.

It is believed that Audrey wrote to each of the next-of-kin of Bob's crew. She received a reply[82] from Wick in the north of Scotland from Moira Stewart, the mother of Sgt. Benjamin C. Stewart, one of the machine-gunners: "We have just had a wire from the Air Ministry saying our son is a POW in Germany and wounded. I do hope and trust you have also had news of your husband ..." She added a PS: "Just this minute got P.C. from Ben. He had slight concussion and was in hospital for 14 days. Came down by parachute. He sounds very cheerful but does not mention rest of crew. I pray you may have equal good fortune."

After her training at OCTU (Officer Cadet Training Unit) at South Wigston in Leicestershire, Audrey was commissioned as 2nd Subaltern (equivalent to 2nd Lieutenant) with effect from 12th May, 1944. She was posted to London and recalled that summer, when it was thought that the War was nearing its end, taking cover from the Nazi "doodlebugs," which were then falling on London.

Around this time, Audrey began to be paid a widow's pension on the basis that Bob was 'missing, presumed dead'. Her application[83] shows that she was recommended for compassionate leave from 19th July to 2nd August, 1944; she had not previously had any leave since 5th November, 1943.

It is thought that it was in September, 1944 that Audrey first heard that Bob was alive after his 'plane had been shot down. Bob's father had received a telephone call from an American soldier named Terzon (or Terzin), who said that he had seen Bob. Bob's father referred to the call in a subsequent letter to Audrey[84] and enclosed a letter[85] from LAC Kenneth Bartlett, who was in the RAF and writing care of the British Liberation Army. The latter explained:

> "...whilst in a café last evening, I met a Belgian who asked me to send news of your son Robert [Bob's name in France and Belgium]. He was in the same prison (camp) in St. Gilles and said he was a good friend of Robert and that he was in good health and as happy as can be expected."

Kenneth Bartlett said the name of the Belgian was Oscar Hupez and enclosed a brief note from him "votre camarade de la prison de St Gilles".[86]

About the same date Audrey received, via Bob's father, a letter[87] from Sergeant F.W. Wilson of the Royal Signals at the Headquarters of the 2nd Army of the British Liberation Army "somewhere in Belgium"; the letter was written in the hope that it might bring "a little consolation and peace of mind." Sgt. Wilson had made friends with two Belgian soldiers and reported that one of them said that "a British sergeant pilot was brought down here"; the Belgian had sheltered the pilot until the Germans came and took him prisoner.

Whilst the Belgian's account does not tally with Bob's own subsequent account, it seems to have brought some encouragement to Audrey, who replied, and Sgt Wilson wrote a further letter[88] to her. He suggested Audrey might visit his wife in Hampton Hill and confided that she had the previous week given birth to a baby girl "and me such a long way away."

A fortnight or so later Audrey received another letter indicating that Bob was in hiding in France after his 'plane was shot down. The letter[89] was written by Lieutenant L.J. Pearce of the RASC petrol depot 135 of the British Liberation Army, who had wrongly assumed that Bob was safely home in England. Audrey apparently wrote explaining the true situation and Lt. Pearce wrote again[90] saying how sorry he was, but "the war is nearly over now and I'm sure it will be only a matter of two or three months before he is back with you again..."

He explained that an order had been made that enabled him to name where the Decayeux family (and others who had helped Bob) lived; it was Cayeux-sur-Mer in the Somme Department. He went on to write that "our good friends helped 21 allied airmen to escape," mentioning especially Mme Decayeux's future sister-in-law, a young woman named Raymonde Monnier.[91] Lt. Pearce was with the first troops to enter Cayeux and he described the scene:

> "...when we reached the town square, a handful of civilians wearing the armband of the F.F.I. [French Forces of the Interior] were waiting to greet us. One or two had rifles, one even had an old steel helmet; a motley crowd at first sight,

but they looked good to me. And at their head, wearing an enormous tricolour ribbon, was little Raymonde. As someone had already told me her story, it was a moving sight. I thought I was a hard-bitten old soldier of over five years, but I confess I was damned near to tears, that day."

The last surviving letters[92][93] from these kind individuals with the British Liberation Army were from Major A.C.O. Greenwood. He wrote of a Willy Fanconnier, whom he had "met at a dinner party (and who held your husband in great esteem)..." Major Greenwood promised if possible to make further enquiries: "There is every possibility of my going back to Belgium and if I can obtain any clues or bits of information I will most certainly let you know."

Audrey meanwhile had been promoted to Subaltern, the A.T.S. equivalent of lieutenant in the Army. In September, 1944, she had attended a course at the School of Pay Duties and in November, 1944 she attended a three-day advanced course at Chatham House on International Affairs.[94]

Audrey had earlier planned to take leave that she had been granted, with a friend, in Edinburgh. The Warden of the Y.W.C.A. there wrote to Audrey that: "Officers are supposed to arrive and leave in uniform but plain clothes may be worn. ...There are no rules about coming in. It is left to the officers' own sense of propriety." [95]

Following a visit by Audrey to the Air Ministry in Oxford Street in October, 1944, a special enquiry about Bob was made of the International Red Cross Committee in Geneva. A letter from the Ministry dated 6ᵗʰ November, 1944[96] reported that a cable from the Red Cross stated that they had no record of Bob as a Prisoner of War. Thus, although Audrey knew in September that Bob had been seen alive in France and Belgium, she did not know whether or not he was still alive over eight months after his 'plane was shot down.

Bob's father kept his elder son, Ted, informed of such news as there was about Bob. Ted was then himself also a POW in Germany and he wrote on 8th November, 1944:[97]

> *I have just received from you the news that Bobbie may still be alive. This has cheered me and lifted me to the heights. ...And you Daddy, keep the old chin up, and shoulders squared, and we will save something yet. It must be a bit of a shock for Audrey, after so long, however let's hope that it is true...*

(Ted had his own war story: he joined the New Zealand Army; was captured at the Battle of El Alamein; was taken as a POW to Italy where he escaped; was sheltered by the Italian Resistance; was re-captured by the Germans and taken to Germany; and was reported to have escaped again from POW camp.)

Above: Bob's photo from his German
POW 'kreigsgefangener' record card.

Below: Metal plate inscribed with Bob's POW number
issued when he was at Stalag Luft VII.

~ CHAPTER IX ~

Stalag Luft VII Bankau

As the Allies advanced following D Day, in August 1944, after over four months in St-Gilles Prison, Bob was transported first to a transit and interrogation camp (Dulag Luft) from where he wrote to Audrey[98] by *Kriegsge-fangenenpost*: "Hullo Darling, I pray this is not the first indication you have had of my safety." (The card was not received by Audrey until late November 1944.) Bob continued: "Please thank the American Red Cross for terrific kindnesses" and in a later letter asks her to send "at least £5" each to the British and American Red Cross.

From the transit camp, Bob (prisoner number 521) arrived, on 11th August, 1944, at Stalag Luft VII, a POW camp opened by the Luftwaffe two months earlier for Non-Commissioned Officers; the prisoners were almost entirely RAF and allied air crew[99]. The camp was situated at Bankau (now Bakow) near to Kreuzburg (now Kluczbork) in Upper Silesia, in what is now Poland.

From Stalag Luft VII Bob wrote in a postcard[100] to his father (also not received until late November): "...Sorry to keep you guessing so long, but am perfectly well. ...I pray that you have news of Ted by now, but if not, do not give up. All my crew, save one, alive I thank God. How's bowling Dad?"

Stalag Luft VII was a great relief at first after St-Gilles Prison and on 12ᵗʰ August[101] Bob wrote to Audrey (this letter and subsequent ones not received until late November or early December): "Hullo my Darling Saturday afternoon in the glorious sunshine & one thanks God one is alive & well." Like so many, he did not expect the War to last much longer:

> *I consider it is not worth your sending any parcels to me even tho' it would give you great happiness, as I shall be home long before they arrive. Had my first pipe a week ago, since coming down – you can guess my childish excitement. Open air & comparative freedom a rare luxury after last few months. Take care Darling, thine, Bob.*

And a few days later: "...We'll have a wizard time this Xmas, I promise, Darling..."[102]

Bob was, however, to some extent putting on a brave face and, in hot weather, wrote in the course of a poem[103] entitled "This Bloody Place" that: "The bloody straw is full of fleas" and:

> *No bloody baths, no bloody showers,*
> *All bloody dust, no bloody flowers...*

A couple of days later Bob seemed in better spirits and wrote to Audrey's Mother, Dorothy Herbst:[104] "... I have just gorged my chocolate ration – yum yum! – & am now enjoying a pipe in the sun. Really I look very healthy thanks to the Red Cross & hope to show off my tan ere long."

The same day, 31ˢᵗ August, 1944, he wrote to Audrey:[105] "...I revel in such a lazy existence, I must confess! Just now I'm in the throes of a bridge tourney... Monday we have a sports day & I have entered for the mile & obstacle races; but really am too lazy to train! Time passes very quickly."

The next sentence was blacked out by censors.

Bob later reported:[106]

> ...Sports Day was grand fun in spite of my sleeping through my obstacle race & coming last in the mile. But enough!! ... Reading & bridge pass the day well, not to mention my efforts at cooking!! Yes – cooking!!!! Wow, am I becoming domesti- cated ...(the next phrase was blacked out by the censor) but still loathe peeling my potatoes.

A notebook written by Bob[107] shows how seriously education was regarded in Stalag Luft VII. Bob himself taught French to fellow prisoners and the notebook gives detailed lesson plans with most lessons beginning with "homework correc- tions". Lesson 12's plan begins "Revise all points brought up by test"!

Other pages include Bob's notes on "The Story of Painting" by Thomas Craven, a copy of Winston Churchill's writing from 1899 entitled "Prisoner of War", lists of books he had read and a list of members of a rugby team in which he was hooker. There is a tabulated timetable showing hour-long lessons on Mondays in Art at 1030 and French (B) at 1800; on Tuesdays in French with Group B at 1345 and Group A at 1800; on Wednesdays Local Government at 1800; on Thurs- days Elocution at 1930 and French (A) at 1915; Fridays Art at 1800; Saturdays French (B) at 1345 and on Sundays two hours'

Architecture beginning at 1030; Bob's notebook includes building plans.

In the next preserved letter, written in October, 1944[108] Bob referred to yet another activity: "...The dancing is coming along fairly well Dear & I promise ... to take you to a dance this winter." He explained that he was writing this in the new winter quarters, "which are comfortable and better". Elsewhere in this letter, he wrote:

> And you my Darling? I pray you are well, not too cheesed & I know you must be getting more beautiful every day. How is the job coming along pet? Any success with our own cottage, flat or room? Boy oh boy, the more I think of our future the happier I feel & I realise so well dearest what a lucky guy I am, having you darling. Whoopee! [the next sentence was censored.]

Bob has still not received any communication from Audrey, but he does not mention this in his letters to her, which remain upbeat:[109]

> ... I am also rugger representative for our division; but as the sports field is not yet ready, that job doesn't entail much. Yes, there is a secret to being content as a POW; & now, so often I feel 24 hours a day is not enough!... Amusing myself lately designing Christmas cards even tho' I expect to be with you by then. Good fun tho'! Well Darling here's the end of this fortnight's ration, ..." [The POWs were at this time allowed to send two letters per month.]

A week later Bob sent Audrey an early Christmas card he had designed.[110]

By 21st November, 1944, Audrey had heard from Bob for the first time in ten months, when she received his letter dated 12th August, 1944.[101] She wrote:[111]

> *My darlingest Bob. Hope some letters have got thru' darling but in case not, all the family are well. ...Can you imagine my hilarious excitement darling but every time we (Beth a new friend from the mess, Jean and I) go out celebrating on your behalf, I wish you had to spend the night popping in and out of bed.*

She goes to describe a room with an attic she has found for them to live in after the War:

> *"...it is in rather a slummy decrepit house with aspidistras in the hall but the old couple are dears and our room looks terribly nice and sunny and gay with lots of cushions, etc. There is a gas ring; and a rickety bowl and stand in the attic to wash in ..." Audrey explains that she is now working in London nearby, which was fortunate "as there has been an enormous amount to do painting, staining and even sewing and hammering."*

Earlier letters which Audrey said she had sent have not survived, and this letter and her subsequent letters were returned to her after the War. Thus Bob, in the whole of his captivity, never received any of Audrey's letters, yet he concealed the disheartenment he must have felt.

Audrey's Mother also wrote to Bob in a letter that was returned[112]: "we are much relieved to know of your safety & that of your crew, alas poor Thomas. A[udrey] has been very brave and has two pips..."

Ironically, the only letter Bob appears to have received as a POW was from his brother Ted in another German prison camp. On 2nd December, 1944 Bob wrote to Audrey[113]: "Hallo Darling, have had my first letter as a POW, and although not from you, it gave me a thrill, particularly to learn from Ted himself that he is somewhere in this country". In the same letter he went on to say that the new theatre "is doing some super entertainment & our first sight of 'Geraldine', the band's blonde bombshell, drove us frantic! ... Had my first game of rugger last week & now hope to play at least once a week."

In this letter Bob also said that he had applied for Ted to join him at Stalag Luft VII! This never happened, but there is indeed a letter which survived[114] from the "Chief British Man of Confidence" on behalf of Bob to the "British Man of Confidence" on behalf of Ted which expressed the "hope that some arrangement may be made whereby the two brothers may finally arrive in the same camp." The letter has a handwritten note in German that it was sent by "Feldpost."

In London Audrey received a letter from the British Red Cross Society and Order of St. John of Jerusalem[115] explaining that letters for Stalag Luft 7 should be sent to Stalag Luft 3 (where letters were censored). Audrey also received instructions for sending parcels[116], which stated that the Board of Trade had authorised an issue of special clothing coupons for clothing sent to POWs in next-of-kin parcels. The Red Cross would "send in every parcel as a gift a ½ lb. slab of plain chocolate." The March 1944 version of the instructions included a special note that "(1) A great quantity of sweets and chocolate is wasted because the Next-of-Kin do not pay attention to the rules regarding chocolate..."

A receipt[117] shows that Audrey paid £2 0s 11d together with 36 coupons for her parcel for Bob; the list of 20 different items includes a pipe, boot polish, 3 pencils and a RAF scarf. However, Bob never received this parcel.

Bob wrote a cheerful and optimistic letter to Audrey on 16th December, 1944,[118] his last surviving war-time letter to her. He reports on his various activities, which include playing rugby: "I've captained the division rugger team twice, as hooker, & we've won both games! It was grand to run around like the old days but rather missed the appropriate beer-up after!" He had also seen "a Mickey Rooney film which was very acceptable..."

In the same letter Bob wrote of teaching Audrey skating and taking her to a dance, having "conquered" the waltz in his prison camp dancing class. He added: "We're making a Christmas Pudding today. Everything OK here Darling so don't worry. We'll have a wizard time soon Pet... Must dash off now Pet to give a French lesson."

Little could Bob and his fellow prisoners have known of the terrible ordeal they were to suffer, which began less than five weeks after this letter was written.

At Christmas, 1944 Audrey was delighted to receive a Christmas card personally signed by her senior "boss", Lord Louis Mountbatten. To Bob she wrote on 18th December, 1944[119] that "everything is getting very Christmassy again darling..." and "Yesterday looking thro' some of your old letters I found the wire you sent me last Christmas Day to Brighton so I shall open it this year and pretend I've just received it!"

Bob was also preparing for Christmas Day 1944 and designed a menu[120], which shows three main meals and three snacks! Dinner was soup followed by venison with baked and mashed potatoes and carrots, with a dessert of Christmas Pudding with cream. The menu is signed in pencil on the back by Bob's room-mates.

In the new year Audrey enquired[121] whether Bob would like anything in particular sent to him as "at the moment I am just sending more or less what the Red X advise." She was pleased to learn of Bob's dancing classes and said she had "wonderful visions of floating around in your arms in a glamorous evening dress and looking like Fred Astaire and Ginger Rodgers."

~ CHAPTER X ~

The Forced March

B ob did not keep a diary during the War, but on 14th February, 1945 he wrote an account of some of his experiences during the previous month. The account is written in pencil in the same notebook[107] that includes his plans for his French lessons; it begins:

Jan 17th 1945. Wednesday
About 11.15 am whilst giving French lesson 22 to two blokes, camp leader came in & told us to be ready to march off in one hour. Rumours were true! Back in 49/12 the food we had was being divided up – and all unpackable & indivisible stuff being consumed at a very fast rate. I joined in heartily. (How we were to regret that in later days!) All ready by one, and told to stand by. Bread and marg – a spot of jerry tinned meat for march dished out. Slept in own clothes that night. Stories of remaining parcels looted etc. The camp was in a disgraceful panic & the whole place literally busted up. Bloody poor show. Terrific air raid nearby during evening.

18th Thur
Whole day spent mooning around - bloody cold – snow - & combines all to cock. Food given now. Out on parade at 6 pm ready to go – then scrubbed again.

19th Fri

Called about 3/5 am & set off, after bags of waiting in the cold, about 7. I had just 2 blankets & a Red Cross box of clothes & food. Hell, how we prayed for end of war – for Joe[122] to catch us. After count & recount we moved off – slow shambling party. Icy roads, snow, biting wind. I had extra clothes on, but no gloves – pretty chilly. Quite a change walking through villages and towns. Bags of refugees in horse carts, army also, made going very slow. Stops occasionally (every 2 hours?) bloody cold. Talked & dreamed of future all time. Partnered with Arthur. Men already falling out with diarrhoea. Pitiful sight. First night spent in very crowded but thank God very warm schoolroom. Most others in barns. Long wait of about 2 hours in freezing cold for billets.

On the page immediately before this account and after the page with the plan for French lesson 24, Bob has written a schedule setting out times and distances in kilometres with occasional extra information. The first day of the march from Bankau to Winterfeld is recorded as 28 km.

20th Saturday

Roused about 6 & moved off again after long wait - until about noon arrived in disused brick works. ½ cup of coffee per man. 5 of us managed to scrounge Red X parcel. I thought of staying behind but after talking over with Arthur decided too risky – not enough food & no one knew where Russians were. Pushed off again at 10 pm in order to cross Oder before bridges blown up. What a grim march! God, how cold – 35 degrees of frost it was said! Bags of blokes dropping out. Could hardly keep ourselves moving – impossible to stop & help them. Crossed the Oder – soldiers guarding mine holes. Waited over hour outside village – then no billets. ...Arrived

in barns about ten o'clock; flopped down too shagged to move.
Bloody cold, dark barn, damp straw.

Bob's schedule states the prisoners had left Winterfeld at 6am on the 20th and arrived at Karlsruhr at 12 noon that day (12kms). They had rested at Karlsruhr until 8pm and marched through the night of 20th/21st, crossing the Oder at 5.30 am, and finally arrived at Rosenfeld at 9am – a distance of 41kms.

The schedule continues:

> 22.1 *[January] Rosenfeld (8am) to Schonfeld (2pm) 21 kms*
> 23.1 *Schonfeld (8am) to Wansen (4pm) 19 kms [rested on 24th]*
> 25.1 *Wansen (8am) to Heiderdorf (4.30pm) 22 kms [rested on 26th]*
> 27.1 *Heiderdorf (11am) to Pfoffendorf (5pm) 21 kms*
> 28.1 *Pfoffendorf (4am) to Standorf (1pm) 13 kms*
> 29.1 *Standorf (5.30pm) to Petrovitz (4.30am) Snowdrifts-very slow going 23 kms [rested until:]*
> 1.2 *Petrowitz (8am) to Prosnitz (2pm) 14 kms*

Bob does not diarize the above part of the March from Rosenfeld to Prosnitz, but gives a general description of these ten gruelling days:

> *... days of shuffling on, with one or two rests. Nights in cold dark, damp crowded barns. Arthur & I in double beds to keep warm. ½ cup of soup daily, little bread and marg. Hot brew very rare. Too cold during day. Frostbite, dysentery etc. One nightmarish night march in blizzard, snowdrifts, blokes dropping out right and left. Tired and hungry, praying, praying for end. Absolutely imposs. to connect this life to*

any other. Was there such a place as home? Would we ever be warm again? Talk of transport. Wait for 3 days ...

On an occasion when Bob mentioned the march, he recalled how it was so cold that his breath froze on his moustache and beard, so that they filled with ice, and that he and his fellow prisoners were at times so thirsty that they used to eat the snow.

Bob also recalled that, during the march, he witnessed a guard shoot dead a prisoner, who had fallen to the ground unable to walk any further. He further mentioned an act of kindness when a German civilian came out of a farmhouse; she gave him and other prisoners potatoes to eat.

The diarised part of Bob's account resumed:

> *Sat Feb 3   took courage and shaved off 2 weeks' beard and moustache, washed all in cup of water!"*

(On 3rd full day at Prosnitz)

> *Sun 4th – Church Service motley throng outside barn gate, hands in pockets, caps on. Wondered what civilians thought as we sang one hymn.*
>
> *Mon Feb 5 – Set off early for Goldberg for transport – ¼ loaf & small pat marg. 8 kms. Fairly pleasant morning. We picked up sugar beet to eat. In train about 10 o'clock. 56 in French cattle wagon. Until Thursday 8th 3 days in that truck – no water – ½ cup coffee – no bread for last 48 hours. Distance only about 180 kms. Deadly in wagon. 2 kms to walk to camp – absolutely starving – could hardly shuffle along. Arrived in [Stalag Luft] IIIA [at Luckenwalde] early afternoon.*

Bob and those fellow prisoners from Stalag Luft VII who survived had marched between 224 and 227 kms in all.

Among other accounts of this forced march is a detailed report dated 15th February, 1945 by D. C. Howatson, RAMC, Camp Medical Officer, and Peter A. Thompson, Pilot Officer, RAAF, Camp Leader[123]. The report was headed: "For the attention of the Swiss Commission, acting as Protecting Power. Report of a Forced March by Occupants of Stalag Luft 7, Germany." It begins:

> *On January 17th 1945, at approximately 11am we received notice of one hour in which to pack our kit and be ready to leave the Camp by marching. At the same time we were informed by Ober Feldwebel Frank that for every one man who fell out of the column on the march, five men would be shot.*

In the course of describing the events of 20th January, the Report stated that at Karlsruhe they were for the first time;

> *"...provided with two field kitchens with which to cook for 1550 men. Each field kitchen was actually capable of cooking sufficient food for 200 men. The Medical Officer was also provided with a horse and cart for the transport of the sick ... the wagon was filled after the first 5 kilometres and from [then] onwards, men were being picked up at the roadsides in a collapsed and frozen state and it was only by sheer willpower that they were able to finish [that day's] march."*

On 21st January, the Report mentioned that at Schonfeld, "Rations issued were about 100 gms. of biscuits per man and half a cup of coffee."

The report of 22nd January began:

> *"At 3am orders were given by the Germans to prepare to march off at once. It was dark and there was some delay in getting the men out from their sleeping quarters because they could not find their baggage. The German guards thereupon marched into the quarters and discharged their firearms."*

The description of events of 5th February, 1945 included:

> *"On arrival at Goldberg we were put into cattle trucks, an average of 55 men to each truck. By this time there were numerous cases of dysentery and facilities for men to attend to personal hygiene were inadequate. The majority had no water on the train journey for two days."*

There are accounts by allied prisoners of war of even harsher forced marches.[124] Why did the Nazis order all these marches requiring numerous soldiers as guards at such a critical time, when they might have easily let the prison camps be overrun by the Russians? One theory is that the Germans feared that the Russians might force the POWs to fight against them. Another theory is that some of the German High Command wanted to use the prisoners as hostages / bargaining counters in peace negotiations.

~ CHAPTER XI ~

Stalag Luft IIIA Luckenwalde

B ob described in his notebook[107] his arrival in the early afternoon of Thursday 8th February, 1945 at Luckenwalde (about 50 kms south of Berlin), the fifth place (if the transit camp is included) where he was imprisoned:

> "Hanging about – then 450 in barrack, on floor, where we are now. Had a wizard lashing of barley soup – Irish compound, blokes very decent, gave us fags. Had a whole Camel – 1st for weeks! What a relief to reach camp, even tho' overcrowded and no Red Cross parcels. Stayed in bed for few days – had tummy trouble – mint tea early morning – soup midday – 1/5 loaf and spuds and sometimes spread and little sugar daily. Arthur and I had little Jerry coffee left thank God.
>
> Sun Feb 11th went to Church. Mon: contacted Les in compound opposite – he gave me 65 cigarettes! Shared with lads and had some tobacco given us."

On 15th February Bob wrote about his day and his feelings at that time:

> "Feel much better now although weak – still too lazy? to wash clothes. See Les twice daily. Get wonderful news bulletin twice daily. Arrange our tea as spuds on toast, with cup coffee. Spend days mainly lying in bed – sometimes reading. Dream

of Audrey & home comforts food and tobacco. War <u>can't</u> last much longer surely! Colossal advances by Russians."

Bob continued his reminisces on a separate piece of paper[125]:

> *"...Often think of my prison life & compare. Got more to eat there – and that seemed not enough! Soup fairly thick today. Jackpot! Wish I could bath and change clothes! Always wishing & dreaming! Just written card to Dad (one to Audrey yesterday) – hope it doesn't sound too bad!"*

Judging by other accounts of the forced march and the conditions at Luckenwalde, Bob played down the deprivation and hardship even in these private notes.

> *"Saw darn good show yesterday given by Irish boys: "Devil Digs Deep" very heavy, but had atmosphere of theatre. Enjoyed pipe of baccy too! Oh for Red Cross parcels! Must see Les now. I personally hope we do not move, at least dry & warm here. Bags of rumours of course ...*

> *8pm Thursday 15th [February] Feel quite contented after our usual supper & have a pipe going. I get a kick of standing round the fire in the Irishmen's room toasting the bread & getting the brew ready. Funny how little things here give such great pleasure.*

> *More memories of the march! Thieving of men's rations.*

> *Feb 23 Friday - 30 parcels divided between 1500 men! and what an exciting day. A draw organised & I drew a 1/5 tin of cheese – Gee what a difference.*

Sat March 3 - ¼ Red Cross parcel! Felt just like a child with new toy! Amazing morale uplift. Cannot describe it – but these notes will suffice.

Sunday morning a cup of coffee with MILK AND SUGAR - first whole cup since Jan 18th. My God what a wonderful luxury. ... Just imagine what a whole parcel would do to us! Oh the end of the war! And going Home!!"

At this time Audrey knew nothing of the forced march. In another letter never received by Bob dated 2nd March 1945[126] it appears Audrey has just received Bob's letter of 16th December, 1944[118], as she jokes:

"Yes sweet, you shall certainly teach me to skate when you come back, but I'm disappointed over the dancing... in fact shall probably send you back again to learn."

Interestingly, it seems that food parcels were also now being received in the UK, as Audrey refers to a "grand" food parcel received from a friend of Ted (Bob's brother), Helen Wake, from New Zealand.

Although the lack of food and water had been even worse on the forced marches, the prisoners at Luckenwalde were suffering from chronic hunger. This is evidenced by Bob's lengthy note headed : "Thursday March 8th 1945 The Great Day!"[127]

"...A writer could make a moving chapter – perhaps a short story – about this issue yesterday. On Wednesday evening everyone was talking, planning and discussing future menus; I was terribly excited and hardly slept at all that night – one

parcel per man! My first complete parcel for myself! Gosh, it brought back vivid memories of Christmas Eve and hanging up the old stocking. Even then there were doubts lingering at the back of my mind. After these six or seven weeks of feeling so very hungry, lying in bed to keep the hunger out, I could hardly imagine the possibilities of a whole American no. 10 to myself. What a thrill it would be to open it up myself!

All that day we sweated on the issue. Would they be able to issue them all (Army, Air Force and also the Yanks)? Would they puncture the tins? That would delay the issue and we'd have to wait until tomorrow. Oh please God let us get them today! ...

Three o'clock, and the Army have gone for theirs! Will we make it? They are definitely UNOPENED!! Thrill upon thrill!

Four! Our blokes are getting 'em now! And so at about 4.30 Thursday March 8th I sat on my blankets with an UNOPENED AMERICAN No. 10 Red Cross parcel between my legs! Arthur by my side. Out with the jolly old razor blade and ....slash! It's opened! What an array of tins!

First, the fags. Good! One hundred Chesterfield. Second, chocolate ... And we, like young school kids, compared our parcels. We had, Arthur & I, lain in bed last night planning, and had decided to pool the fags and choc. plus any other different commodities for variety sake, but to keep our spreads etc. so that we could each eat when and what we liked. ... I had 2 tins of salmon, Arthur 2 of sardines, hence one of each for both of us.

And so we settled ourselves, amidst a cloud of blue smoke. Gosh, what a hubbub! Could Jerry get us on roll call? Could he hell! Before I give a list of what remained in my Prize Box, I feel I must mention one very disagreeable point. It was just plain bloody awful to see so many bods carrying their parcels on parade for fear of having them stolen. There has been a *helluva lot of pilfering. Already I hear of two parcels being pinched last night! Senior NCOs !! ....*

Strange how I have begun to like smoking cigs. Do hope that my love for my pipe does not disappear entirely, but don't think it will be, when I get a decent pipe and some tobacco.

Couldn't sleep very well during early hours. How enjoyable to reach for a cigarette!

I think that's about the lot. The joy of diving into my box is still there – and strong rumours of another parcel, this time Canadian, on Monday!! But let's wait and see, for I am perfectly content with this life now."

Audrey, meanwhile, received a card from Bob written from Luckenwalde,[128] which she acknowledges in a letter to him dated 10th April, 1945.[129] She writes from 58 Abingdon Villas, Kensington, W8: "...Anyhow darling the larder is well stocked & our little room... is ready waiting for us to start our life of domestic bliss..." In a PS Audrey tells Bob that he has been promoted to Flight Sergeant.

Bob's own surviving writings get briefer, the next note, dated Saturday, 21st April, 1945 simply stating: "Goons sheared off."[130]

Bob &
Audrey's
War

~ CHAPTER XII ~

Liberation

Bob's note for Sunday 22nd April, 1945 reads:

> *"Russians arrived. Increase of rations for few days. Food scarce. Waiting, waiting, waiting..."*

THIS WAS NO ORDINARY liberation. Bob said that the Russian soldiers were often ill-disciplined and even stole watches from Allied prisoners.[131] Their behaviour was to an extent understandable given the suffering of so many Russian armies. Indeed, it is believed that 2,000 to 2,500 Soviet POWs had died at Luckenwalde in the winter of 1941/1942.[132]

Later, the consensus view developed that the Russians were, in effect, holding the Allied POWs as hostages. The Red Army had "clear instructions not to let the British and American prisoners go home until Stalin was certain he had cemented his control of Poland."[133]

On the back of a postcard of an open-air swimming pool[134] Bob recorded that, on 3rd May, 1945, he went with an Advance Party to a camp a few miles south-west of Luckenwalde, "as French interpreter!!" Returning two days later, he wrote: "Wizard little room, shared with Vic Cooper. Beautiful camp, but spoiled by looting." He also mentioned that there were "hordes of hungry refugees".

Bob's cryptic note written about the days following his return to Luckenwalde, reads: "First Big Panic. Red Cross Ambulances arrived for sick. Lorries following 6.5.45? ...Russian authorities snooty."

Light is shed on Bob's note in the written account by the Senior British Officer at Stalag IIIA to the Russian Commandant for Repatriation there (dated 7th May, 1945) of what he said at a conference on 6th May:[130]

>...From 22nd April, I, at the request of the Russian Authorities, have been responsible for the administration and security of this entire camp of 16,000 mixed nationalities. The work of the camp during this time has been carried out mainly by British and American officers and men. It should, however, be appreciated that, owing to the Russian orders re confinement to camp etc., we have had to continue for all intents and purposes as prisoners. ... It is important to understand and make allowances for the mental attitude of prisoners of war who have been liberated but are still denied their freedom.
>
> The food situation, up to yesterday, was precarious, and the daily ration, even though assisted by American supplies, is still grossly inadequate. ... Furthermore, the camp has become even more overcrowded owing to the influx of Italian refugees. The problems of sanitation are considerable, and the general health is threatened. ...
>
> Yesterday the American representative from Supreme Allied Headquarters returned with a convoy to carry out his orders [to evacuate the Americans and British in that order]. Capt. Tchekanov ... refused to allow him to proceed with his duties. Later, when an attempt was made to proceed with the evacuation, armed force was used against American troops

to prevent their leaving the camp. ... In spite of continual assurances that we were to be repatriated with the least possible delay, we now see the Russians actively preventing such repatriation. ...

On the day this account was written, Bob subsequently wrote: "Several lorries went with many blokes unofficially." Bob, however, continued to follow the Russian orders (which POWs were advised to adhere to for their own safety) to remain in camp.

Bob's next note reads: "Tues 8.5. War over. No thrill at all. 2 attempts to evacuate unsuccessful. Arthur got away." Despite Bob's feeling of anticlimax on the end of the war in Europe, he treasured his copies of the V.E.Day speeches of Winston Churchill[135] and King George VI[136] circulated at Luckenwalde.

On 11th May, 1945 Bob wrote: "Settled down now to wait," but the next day he recorded: "Moved to Iruppenlager".

In his pencil notes for later in May, 1945 (written on his copy of Churchill's speech[135]) Bob recorded:

Monday 14th – Our Wedding Anniversary !!

Sunday 20th. Sudden panic! Moved off at about midday. Broken journey owing to demolished bridges on autobahns. Met Yanks at Elbe. On to Halle. What a supper!

Monday 21st WHIT MONDAY - On fatigues in cookhouse at 6 am! Who cares? We're going home!!! Oh Darling Audrey! Wizard food ... Hot showers!!"

The POWs received a card from the British and Common-wealth Red Cross[137] declaring: "We Salute You and wish you the very Best of Luck". On the reverse Bob wrote WHIT

MONDAY with a list of what he had received: "1/4 lb chocolate. Pkt Edgeworth tobacco. 1 pipe. Toothbrush. 2 handkerchiefs. pkt chewing gum"

Next day Bob recorded: "Wonderful rations again."

On Friday 25th May Bob reached No. 1 Canadian Transit Camp (X PW) at Brussels. The Commanding Officer's welcome sheet[138] stated the object was "to make you as comfortable as possible and to provide an early return to 'Blighty.'" The Reception Drill included a medical inspection, a "dusting" (presumably de-lousing) and interrogation on a voluntary basis.

The recreational facilities at this transit camp included a "Dry Canteen" with ping-pong, "dance bands or other music" etc. In the "Wet Canteen" the beer was "only a fair substitute for 'Mild and Bitter.'"

Bob noted that he left the Canadian Transit Camp next day (on 26th May), although it seems to have been a few days before he was repatriated.

There is no written account of the next month, but Audrey said that she and Bob had three ecstatic days in their "love-nest" in Abingdon Villas in Kensington. Family and friends agreed to stay away during this period!

Audrey also said that, despite the good food Bob received during his last few days on the Continent, he weighed less than 6 stones (38 kg) when they were re-united.[139]

~ CHAPTER XIII ~

Demob

I t is recorded that Bob returned from "overseas service" on 1st June, 1945.[140] On 25th July 1945 Bob, now Warrant Officer Kenyon-Ormrod, appeared before a Medical Board at RAF Cosford in Shropshire and, perhaps surprisingly in view of his weight less than a couple of months before, was given medical classification "A/B".[141]

It is believed that it was very shortly after this that Bob and Audrey had their "third" honeymoon[142] as Audrey had promised – at Holywell Bay in Cornwall.

On 4th August, 1945 Audrey "was struck off unit strength" at the London Military Dispersal Unit with release leave to 29th September. She received a letter[143] with the thanks of the Army Council for "the valuable services which you have rendered in the service of your country at a time of grave national emergency." On her relinquishing her commission she was granted the honorary rank of Subaltern.

Uniquely, among Bob's papers are newspaper cuttings[144] relating to the court martial in August, 1945 of Raymond Davies Hughes, who collaborated with the Nazis and was accused of broadcasting, in Welsh, anti-Jewish propaganda directed at Welsh troops; he was allegedly assisted in his writing by William Joyce's wife. (Hughes escaped the death penalty and was sentenced to five years' hard labour subsequently reduced to two years.) After Hughes had collaborated with the Nazis in Berlin, the Germans decided to move him away.

In August 1944 he arrived at Stalag Luft VII. A couple of months later Hughes was suspected of giving the Germans details of an escape tunnel at the camp. He was arrested by fellow prisoners and brought before a 'court' in the Camp Leader's room, when "he broke down." After a night under POW guard,

> "...the Camp Leader and Man of Confidence decided that, as the Germans might take reprisals, it would be best if Hughes were handed back to the Germans and so the wretched man was escorted to the main gate, accompanied by most of the camp."[145]

Bob's "Service and Release Book"[140] shows that in September 1945 Bob was back at RAF Cosford Dispersal Centre in Shropshire. He was granted release, his character being described as "Very Good," the highest category.

As standard practice, Bob was relegated to the RAF Reserve. One of the conditions was that he should preserve his uniform "in good condition in case of recall." Bob was granted 80 days' paid leave expiring on 1st December, 1945.

After the War, Bob hankered after flying again and in 1950 he applied to join the Royal Air Force Volunteer Reserve for five years' service.[146] For some reason unknown, this application was not pursued, but Bob applied again in 1952. He was told that he was too old at the age of 35 for the RAFVR without special qualifications, which he did not have.[147]

Thwarted in his wish to fly aeroplanes, Bob took up lessons to fly gliders at Lasham Gliding Club and enthused about this pastime. He could not, however, on his salary afford to continue this expensive hobby.

Bob &
Audrey's
War

Epilogue

After demobilisation, Bob took up the place, for which he had been accepted before the War, at Borough Road Teachers' Training College in Isleworth. He specialized in French and Art.

Son David was born on 5th May, 1946. After he and his mother were discharged from St Thomas's Hospital, the family lived at 105 Abingdon Road, Kensington, W8, just around the corner from the "love-nest" that Audrey had prepared for Bob's return after his imprisonment as a POW.

Despite his war-time experiences, Bob continued to enjoy travelling on the Continent and in 1948 took Audrey and David to Paris, where they met up with his sisters, Dods and Edwina. Bob returned to Picardy, where he was welcomed by some members of the Resistance who had sheltered him during the War. He learnt that in one village where he had stayed, twenty airmen had been hidden by the Resistance and that, as a punishment, the Nazis made the women and children stand in the village square for 24 hours.

On another holiday in the 1950s, in Amsterdam, Bob jumped clothed into a canal to save a boy who had fallen in.

Meanwhile, daughter Kate was born on 3rd July, 1949 in Petts Wood (now in Greater London) and son John was born on 15th February, 1963 in Caversham, Reading. Kate would become a social worker, John a clinical psychologist, and David a solicitor. Not only did Bob and Audrey provide a loving and stable home for their children, but they were also good friends to very many. During the early 1950s, Audrey additionally made time to train and become a voluntary Red Cross hospital nurse.

Bob first taught in secondary schools before switching to primary education. In 1951 he became "first assistant master" on the opening of a new school, Red Hill Junior School in Chislehurst, which was then in Kent. Bob painted a large, detailed pictorial map of Kent across the full length of a wall in the entrance hall, which stood for many years.

In 1956 Bob was appointed headteacher of Battle Junior School in Reading and in 1962 became the first head of a new school in Tilehurst, Reading – Churchend Primary School. While he was there, he suffered a heart attack and, although he returned as headteacher, took early retirement in 1978.

In retirement Bob turned his creative talent to wood-turning and loved to display and sell his beautiful bowls and other objects at craft fairs.

Meanwhile, Audrey developed her creative talent in embroidery – mainly cross stitch. She led workshops around the country and exhibited, usually with friends, in Henley-on-Thames, at Foyles Bookshop in London and elsewhere. Her "Hands" wall hanging, dedicated to prisoners of conscience, can be seen in the church of All Hallows-by-the-Tower in the City of London.

Bob was keen to live in a more rural area and he and Audrey moved to live on the edge of Corsham in Wiltshire in 1987. While Bob built a workshop at their new home, Audrey completed the writing of her book *Exploring Cross Stitch*.[148]

Sadly, it was not long after moving to Corsham that Bob developed cancer. Nevertheless, during a period of remission, he continued to enjoy driving and he became a member of a local charity, driving residents to hospital and doctors' surgeries. This was, however, short-lived, as his cancer spread. Bob died on 11th September, 1989, aged 71.

In 1990 Audrey returned to Caversham, Reading, where she had a wide circle of friends. She continued her embroidery, expanding into collage and painting. She died in Plymouth on 14th June 2012, aged 90.

Bob &
Audrey's
War

NOTES

WHERE NO REFERENCE IS shown for the source of my writing about an event or giving a description, the source is either my own conversations with Bob or Audrey, or a matter of public record.

[1] Soldier's Service and (second) Pay Book.

[2] Army Form A2022, headed "Anti-Gas."

[3] In a conversation with me on 3.9.89, during the 50th anniversary commemorations of the outbreak of World War II, just eight days before Bob died.

[4] The cutting is undated, although Bob's handwritten note reads "1940ish."

[5] They remain, and serve as the road link between the islands and the mainland.

[6] Airman's Service and Pay Book.

[7] Travelling instructions from Kensington Palace Barracks.

[8] Parliament Hill School Magazine, 1957, written following the retirement of the much-loved headmistress, Miss Edmed.

[9] The telegram is dated 17th April, 1941. Audrey spoke of seeing the crashed 'plane, but I cannot recall whether any of the crew survived.

[10] Audrey's Soldier's Service and Pay Book.

[11] Certified List of this date.

[12] Her own war records.

[13] These telegrams were attached, framed and hung on the "playroom" wall of our family home until about 1970. Also attached (out of view) is a congratulatory letter from Bob's sister, Dorothy, dated 29.3.42.

[14] After Bob's death, Audrey recounted how, on the evening of their wedding day, Bob was apprehensive and questioned whether they had rushed into marriage. Audrey reassured Bob and said

that, whatever happened, they would support each other through the challenges of war-time and beyond.

[15] Bob's surviving R.A.F. records are extremely limited, but Bob kept his Royal Canadian Air Force "Pilot's Flying Log Book," which has a complete record of his service and the aircraft he flew.

[16] Recorded in Bob's "Pilot Flight Record and Log Book," issued by the Aviation Supply Corporation of Georgia, which copies much of the material in the full "Pilot's Flying Log Book."

[17] Under this scheme, named after its American innovator General Arnold, British pilots and navigators were sent to be trained with American cadets by the U.S. Army Air Corps. Interestingly, the scheme petered out in 1942 because of the high failure rate among British recruits, due to their poor level of scientific education. ("The Arnold Scheme: British Pilots, the American South and the Allies' Daring Plan" by Gilbert Guinn (Spellmount (Publishers) Ltd.) at pp. 484 and 541)

[18] Letter written on his father's birthday.

[19] Undated letter numbered 3.

[20] The Airgraph is dated 12.6.42 and is addressed to Audrey in Marlow, Bucks., where she was then billeted.

[21] Letter from Leading Aircraftman H. Kenyon-Ormrod, 2 Squadron, dated 15.6.42.

[22] Airgraph dated 22.6.42.

[23] Third letter dated 3.7.42.

[24] Bob has written on the back of the menu the route via Toronto, Detroit, Cincinnati and Atlanta.

[25] Letter numbered 4 from Georgia, dated 13.7.42 with the Moncton address as the correspondence address, as Bob had been instructed.

[26] V...-Mail letter dated 26.7.42. It is possible that this letter never left North America, as there is no evidence that it was reduced to photographic form, whereupon the original would normally have been destroyed, according to the printed V...-Mail instructions.

[27] Long letter dated 3.8.42.

[28] Another long letter, dated 7.9.42.

[29] I was told about this letter by Audrey.

[30] When I toured America in the summer of 1967, I received the same welcome and hospitality from these three families. The Carswell and Harrison families still lived in the same towns, but the Brooks family had by then moved to Gilmer, Texas. Bob remained in contact with all of them long after the War. From childhood days, I well remember the huge parcel of presents and luxuries we received from John and Lita Brooks every Christmas.

[31] Certified entries in his log book.

[32] Combat manoeuvres from the First World War.

[33] The certificate bears a cartoon and is headed "Blind Flight."

[34] This diploma certificate is dated "this twenty-sixth day of February in the year of our Lord one thousand nine hundred and forty-three."

[35] Telegram received in Maidenhead, Berks. that day.

[36] The receipted bill from R.J. Connors.

[37] Letter headed "Chipping Norton, Tuesday afternoon."

[38] First published by John Castle, September 1924. Wilfred Partington's friend, H.V. Morton, wrote of this book on 22nd September, 1924: "Dear Parti, You've got to accept my congratulations on the tobacco book, whose conception six centuries ago I remember......"

[39] Slightly damaged telegram. Audrey's war records state that she was made Acting Corporal in May and Corporal in August.

[40] After the War, the station was transferred to Coastal Command and during the Cold War was a base for anti-submarine duties, later becoming the home of Nimrod maritime patrol aircraft. (Guy Jefferson at ForresWeb)

[41] No letters remain from this period when Bob was in Scotland.

[42] "R.A.F. Bomber Command 1939-45" edited by Jonathan Falconer [2018] at p. 58 (Hayes Publishing).

[43] Certificate in Bob's Flying Log Book.

[44] There is a pigeon cage in the reconstructed Halifax at the York Air Museum, at the former R.A.F. Station at Elvington. Incidentally,

there is only one other surviving Halifax, which is at the National Air Force Museum of Canada in Trenton, Ontario.

[45] Philip J.R. Moyes writing in the September 1984 edition of "Planes."

[46] On the second anniversary of Bob and Audrey's first meeting.

[47] Bob also wrote that he was relieved to find out that Audrey was home from hospital. It is not known why she had been admitted to hospital.

[48] It is signed on the reverse by four of Bob's crew.

[49] Letter dated 31.1.44.

[50] Letter dated simply "Wednesday."

[51] Letter headed "Friday."

[52] Letter dated 15.2.44 with his R.A.F. Burn address.

[53] This letter is headed "Saturday" and, from its contents, would seem to have been written on 19.2.44.

[54] This is an abbreviated account of the raid on Leipzig in the highly detailed book about Halifax aircraft and their role in the War and after, which is entitled "Handley Page Halifax from Hell to Victory and Beyond" by K.A. Merrick (Ian Allan Publishing) at p. 66.

[55] Letter of this date from R.A.F. Burn.

[56] From the authoritative 2013 book "The Bombing War; Europe 1939-1945" by Richard Overy (Penguin) at pp. 367/8.

[57] Taken from the booklet prepared by Michel Decelle (President of the Association des Sauveteurs d'Aviateurs Allies) for the Mayor and Council of Cahon and for my wife Helen and me, on the occasion of our visit to Cahon on 12.11. 2015.

[58] Merrick at p. 114 – cited at [54].

[59] Overy at p. 349 – cited at [56].

[60] On 12.11.2015, Helen and I were privileged to be taken there by the Mayor of Cahon and Serge Tavernier (who saw the crashed 'plane as a small boy) together with Xavier de Groulard, and other members of Cahon Council, and Michel Decelle referred to above [57].

⁶¹ Copy of translated letter on behalf of Alexandre Mangeot to the War Office dated 20.10.47 (subsequently confirmed by Bob).

⁶² Copy of translated letter from Julien Toron to the War Office dated 18.11.47 (likewise confirmed by Bob).

⁶³ Not only did Bob himself tell me about this, but Helen and I were delighted to meet Gérard and Michel, who gave us their recollections. We met on Armistice Day, 2015, when I was honoured to lay a bouquet at the Memorial to the Allied Soldiers at Cayeux-sur-Mer. In the course of our tour of the area, Gérard showed us his parents' home in St. Valery-sur-Somme. The current owner took us through his home to the back yard, from which we saw the window of the bedroom Bob shared with the boys, who later escaped from this window when the Nazis were searching for their father.

⁶⁴ His business card and letter from the War Office dated 15.10.47. Bob subsequently confirmed the assistance given by M. Ricard.

⁶⁵ Mary McCall of Wanlockhead, Dumfricsshire to Audrey dated 16.12.44.

⁶⁶ The national newspaper "News Chronicle" ran a competition for ex-service readers called "Let's Go Back" inviting them to write, in under 250 words, about a war-time experience. These are extracts from Bob's letter dated 2.7.51, which was published on 9.7.51, but did not win the competition.

⁶⁷ Bob's fuller draft letter to the "News Chronicle" dated 1.7.51, which was over the word limit of the newspaper's competition.

⁶⁸ 8 photos inscribed by Arlette, including several of Bob with the Baillet family, which reached England via the French Red Cross, with a letter dated 21.10.45.

⁶⁹ Postcard dated 30.10.44.

⁷⁰ The above postcard and a letter from Arlette dated 9.6.45 are all that have survived.

⁷¹ Letter from Julien Toron to Bob dated 18.11.47.

⁷² Conversations with Gérard and Michel on 11.11.2015.

⁷³ On the same sheet from a notebook as his poem quoted below.

⁷⁴ The poem headed "Solitary" is dated 24.5.44.

75 Telegram dated 25.2.44.

76 Undated note found with Bob's letter to Audrey dated 22.2.44.

77 Letter from the Casualty Branch dated 5.3.44.

78 Headed "Confidential Notice."

79 "Advice to the Relative of a Man who is Missing."

80 The letter is signed by Leslie Fawcett on his behalf.

81 Letter dated 20.3.44 signed on behalf of the Wing Commander.

82 Letter dated 20.4.44.

83 Application for Leave of Absence.

84 Letter dated 22.9.44. Whilst Audrey told me of this call, I do not recall any details, other than that his name was Terzin. His name is mentioned later in a letter from the Air Ministry.

85 Letter dated 14.9.44.

86 The note from Oscar Hupez.

87 Letter dated 13.9.44, written in faint pencil.

88 Letter dated 26.9.44.

89 Letter dated 8.10.44.

90 Long letter dated 26.10.44.

91 On 11.11. 2015 Helen and I were delighted to meet Raymonde's daughter, Sylvie Nolbert, and Sylvie's half-sister, Christiane Decayeux, granddaughter of Paul and Elisma Decayeux, who had helped Bob.

92 Undated letter addressed to Bob.

93 The later letter to Audrey is dated 3.11.44.

94 Extracted from Audrey's war records.

95 Young Women's Christian Association of Great Britain, dated 18.10.44.

96 Following letters from the Air Ministry dated 25.10.44 and 3.11.44 (missing).

97 Letter from Ted to their father of this date.

98 Postcard dated 6.8.44.

99 In their book "The Long Road" Oliver Clutton-Brock and

Raymond Crompton (Grub Street 2013) describe the camp and chronicle events there in detail, and also record numerous prisoners' accounts of their experiences – many grim - before their capture.

[100] Postcard dated 12.8.44.

[101] Letter of this date passed by both German and British censors (as were the postcards).

[102] Postcard dated 17.8.44.

[103] The poem is dated 29.8.44.

[104] Postcard dated 31.8.44.

[105] Letter of this date, received by Audrey in December.

[106] Letter to Audrey dated 14.9.44.

[107] The notebook has in its heading a note written on 15.2.45 that it was "begun about middle October 1944."

[108] Letter dated 17.10.44.

[109] Letter dated 31.10.44.

[110] Card dated 7.11.44.

[111] Letter from Audrey dated "21", which the postmark confirms was November 1944.

[112] Letter from Dorothy Herbst dated 28.11.44.

[113] Letter of this date, marked in German by Bob "by air mail."

[114] Dated 12.12.44 and signed by A.D. Neale.

[115] Letter dated 12.12.44 with enclosed note.

[116] Dated March 1943 together with amendment and March 1944 revision.

[117] The list and receipt are headed "Joint War Organisation B.R.C.S. & S.J.A.B." and dated 8.1.45.

[118] Although the letter is dated 16.12.44, it was not received by Audrey until late February 1945.

[119] Another of Audrey's letters in the series not received by Bob and returned to her after the War.

[120] The menu also states "Room 12 Block 49 Stalag L.7."

[121] Returned letter dated 12.1.45.

[122] The Russians were rapidly advancing and this would be a reference to Joseph Stalin.

[123] A typed copy of this report contains a note by Bob that he was given it on 28.4.85 at the Service of Commemoration at St. Clements Dane by Pat Doolan, who was also on this march.

[124] See, for example, the highly researched book by John Nichol and Tony Rennell: "The Last Escape; The Untold Story of Allied Prisoners of War in Germany 1944-45" (Viking). There is a brief account of Bob's march from Stalag Luft VII on pp. 167-8. There is also a detailed account of the march in "The Long Road." [99]

[125] A page torn from a different notebook.

[126] Letter of this date returned after the War.

[127] It is dated 9.3.45 and written on P.O.W. notepaper.

[128] This has not survived.

[129] Not received by Bob, and returned to Audrey after the War.

[130] Written, as are Bob's following notes, on a duplicated copy of the typed complaint from the Senior British Officer at Stalag IIIA to the Russian Commandant for Repatriation at Stalag IIIA.

[131] The first time I heard Bob mention this was in a conversation I overheard when I was aged 8 or 9. Taking such incidents out of context, I vividly remember, in a classroom discussion about the Second World War (at Red Hill County Primary School, Chisle-hurst), that I piped up: " The Russians were even worse than the Germans." I was gently corrected by the teacher, whose name was Marion. [Bob was Deputy Head at the same school. He and Audrey were very sociable, and I used to see members of staff at our home, and hence I remember only her Christian name.]

[132] Literature at Stalag IIIA Luckenwalde cemetery and exhibition.

[133] "The Last Escape" [124] at p.214.

[134] The Adolf Hitler Baths at Lager bei Juterbog.

[135] Delivered at 16.00 hours.

[136] Headed "The King's Speech."

[137] With "Best Wishes for a Happy Return Home."

[138] It concludes: "BEST OF LUCK, GOD BLESS."

[139] Bob weighed 9 stone when he first went to Bankau according to his own note.

[140] His R.A.F. Service and Release Book certificate page.

[141] Copy summary certificate of this date on Form 657.

[142] Their "first" honeymoon was a few days in Henley-on-Thames after their wedding on 14.5.42 and the "second" is thought to be the week's holiday in Harrogate after Bob's return from North America.

[143] Formal letter from the War Office dated 19.9.45

[144] 2 of 3 cuttings are from "The Morning Post."

[145] "The Long Road" at p.182.

[146] Notice Paper dated 20.7.50.

[147] Letter from the Commandant of No.4 R.A.F. Reserve Centre dated 12.6.52.

[148] First published by A & C Black (Publishers) Ltd in 1988. Copyright David Ormrod 2021.

Bob &
Audrey's
War